LUCY DANIELS
Chick
Challenge

Illustrated by Paul Howard

**Hodder
Children's
Books**

a division of Hodder Headline plc

Special thanks to Helen Magee
Thanks also to C. J. Hall, B.Vet.Med., M.R.C.V.S., for reviewing
the veterinary material contained in this book.

Copyright © 1996 Ben M. Baglio
Created by Ben M. Baglio, London W6 0HE
Illustrations copyright © 1996 Paul Howard
Cover illustration by Chris Chapman

First published in Great Britain in 1997
by Hodder Children's Books

A Catalogue record for this book is available from the British Library

ISBN 0 340 68730 4

Typeset by Avon Dataset Ltd, Bidford-on-Avon, Warks

Printed and bound in Great Britain by
Mackays of Chatham PLC, Chatham, Kent

Hodder Children's Books
a division of Hodder Headline plc
338 Euston Road
London NW1 3BH

Contents

1

A new arrival

"I'm *so* excited about Duchess's kittens," Mandy Hope said to James Hunter as they walked along Welford's main street to school.

James smiled. "You get excited about all the animals that come to Animal Ark," he said.

Mandy's parents were both vets in Welford. Their surgery was at the back of Animal Ark, the stone cottage where Mandy and her parents lived.

"But it's *always* exciting," Mandy said. "I think it must be much more interesting looking after animals than people. I mean, people are all the same. Animals are all different."

"Like four-legged ones and two-legged ones," said James.

"And some with no legs at all," said Mandy. "Like Gertie, Gary's garter-snake."

Gary Roberts was in Mandy's class at Welford Primary School. He had a pet garter-snake. Mandy always took a great interest in the pets of her school-friends.

"Duchess was in for a check-up yesterday," she said. "Her kittens are due any time now."

Duchess was Richard Tanner's Persian cat and this was her very first litter. Richard was also in Mandy's class.

James hitched his schoolbag on to his

shoulder. "You'd rather have animals than people any day, Mandy," he said.

Mandy grinned. She loved going home every day to find out what new animals had arrived at Animal Ark.

"Dad says that too," she said. "In fact, so does Mum!"

"So does *everybody*!" said James.

Mandy laughed. James was her best friend. He was in the class below her at school – and he liked animals almost as much as she did. "You should talk!" she said.

"So," said Mrs Todd at the end of afternoon school. "You've all got to think about what we're going to do at Easter. Let's have your ideas. You've usually got plenty." She looked at Mandy. "Oh, Mandy, Mrs Garvie wants to see you. You can go along now."

"Me?" said Mandy, surprised. Mrs Garvie was the Headteacher of Welford Primary School.

"Don't worry," said Mrs Todd. "There's something she wants you to help her with. You aren't in any trouble."

The Headteacher's door was open when Mandy arrived. Mrs Garvie turned to her and smiled. There was a little girl standing beside her. She had dark curly hair and looked about five years old.

"Come in, Mandy," Mrs Garvie said. She looked at the little girl. "This is Libby Masters," she went on. "She lives at Blackheath Farm up on the moor and

she's had to start school late in the term. I'd like you to look after her for me."

Mandy looked at Libby and smiled. "Of course I will," she said to Mrs Garvie.

Mrs Garvie smiled at Libby. "I told you we could rely on Mandy," she said. "I'm sure she'll take good care of you." Then she turned to Mandy again. "Libby's mum is coming to collect her soon," she said. "Why don't you get to know each other in the meantime?"

Mandy nodded. "Let's go and find James," she said to Libby. "You'll like him. He's got a black Labrador called Blackie and a cat called Benji. Do you like animals?"

Libby nodded, but Mandy could see her bottom lip trembling as she followed Mandy out of the Headteacher's room.

"Do you have any pets?" she asked gently.

"You mean, like a dog or a cat?" said Libby. She shook her head.

"Never mind," said Mandy. "You live

on a farm, so there must be lots of animals around. You don't need to have a pet of your own."

The bell for end of school rang as they came out into the playground.

"Do *you* have a pet?" Libby asked.

Mandy smiled and shook her head. "I'm like you," she said. "My mum and dad are vets so there are always lots of animals around, but I don't have a special pet of my own."

"Hi! Mandy!" called a voice.

Mandy looked up. "There's James," she said.

James ran up to them, his face flushed. "Have you heard about the fancy dress party?" he asked.

Mandy shook her head.

James grinned. "It was Laura Baker's idea," he said. "Mrs Black was talking about what we would do for Easter. We had a picnic last year, remember?"

"I like rolling eggs at Easter," Libby said.

Mandy gave Libby a quick look. She looked a lot more cheerful.

"This is Libby Masters, James," she said. "I told Mrs Garvie we'd look after her for a few days. She just started school today."

James grinned at Libby. "What was your last school like?" he said.

Libby bit her lip. "I didn't go to school," she said. "I couldn't start. I had a broken leg."

James looked sympathetic. "That was rotten luck," he said. "It isn't easy starting late, is it?"

Libby looked grateful. "Oh, no," she said. "It's really hard."

"Was your leg very sore?" Mandy asked.

Libby shook her head. "Only at first," she said. "But I couldn't run about."

"You must have been lonely," Mandy said.

Libby nodded and her eyes lit up for a moment. "I had Ronda," she said.

Mandy was just going to ask who Ronda was when Laura Baker came running up.

"Did James tell you about the Easter party?" she said to Mandy. "It's fancy dress. Jack Gardiner and I are going to go as Easter bunnies. We're going to make bunny masks with big front teeth and huge ears. What will you go as, Mandy?"

Mandy laughed. "I've only just heard about it!" she said.

"Isn't it great that Jack and I both have rabbits?" Laura said. "Mrs Black says we can bring them with us to the party."

James's face lit up. "Does that mean I can take Blackie?" he said.

"Blackie would love to come," said Mandy.

"You could make him an Easter bonnet," Laura said, giggling.

"I don't think Blackie would like that very much," James said.

"You'll really enjoy the Easter party,

Libby," Mandy said to the little girl.

"What kind of mask are you going to make?" Laura asked Libby.

"Libby hasn't got a pet," said Mandy, "so she could choose any kind of mask – like me."

"You could come as a rabbit, with Jack and me," Laura said. "I've got three of them – Nibbles, Patch and Fluffy. You could carry Patch if you like. He's very friendly and rabbits are really Eastery."

James grinned. "*Eastery*," he said. "I like that. What else is Eastery?"

"Chickens," Mandy said. "Little Easter chicks."

James looked at Libby. "There you are then, Libby," he said. "You and Mandy could go as Easter chickens. You could make chick masks."

Mandy turned eagerly to Libby. The little girl's eyes were fixed on James. Suddenly her bottom lip began to tremble and her eyes filled with tears. Mandy reached out a hand to her but she turned

away. Libby ran across the playground to the school gate. Mandy watched as a car drew up and a woman got out. Libby ran right into her arms.

"Wow!" said James. "What did I say?"

Mandy frowned, her eyes on the car as it drew away from the school gates. "I don't know, James," she said. "I'm sure you didn't say anything to upset her."

James shoved his glasses up his nose. "I hope not," he said. "Poor kid. She really does seem unhappy, doesn't she?"

Mandy nodded. "Yes, she does," she said. "And I wish I knew why."

2

Who is Ronda?

Mandy waited patiently at the school gate next morning. She wanted to be there when Libby's mum dropped her off. When the car drew up, Libby gave her a big smile and Mandy relaxed. This morning the little girl seemed fine.

Libby's mum got out and came to the

gate with her daughter. Mandy smiled up at her.

"You must be Mandy," Mrs Masters said. "Libby has told me all about you – and your friend James. You've been really kind to Libby."

Mandy blushed. "It's really hard to start school late," she said.

Mrs Masters nodded. "I know," she said. "Everybody has made friends already. I think Libby feels a little left out. It's a pity. We were really look-ing forward to Libby making lots of friends at school. Our farm is so isolated. She hardly ever sees other children."

Mandy looked at Libby and smiled. "You'll soon have lots of friends, Libby. You'll see," she said.

Mrs Masters gave Libby a quick hug and drove off. Mandy and Libby walked through the school gates together.

"Don't you have anybody at all to play with at home?" asked Mandy.

Libby thought for a moment. "I've got Ronda," she said.

"What's Ronda like?" Mandy said, interested.

Libby's head drooped. "She's got a lovely red coat," she said and her mouth turned down.

Mandy changed the subject. It seemed that thinking about her friend, Ronda, made the little girl sad. If only she knew why.

She and James puzzled over Ronda during the rest of the week.

"I wonder what it is about Ronda that makes her so sad," Mandy said on their way home from school on Wednesday.

"Ask her," said James.

Mandy shook her head. "I don't want to upset Libby," she said. "I mean, maybe her friend is moving away or maybe she's ill. But every time she mentions Ronda she nearly starts to cry."

James nodded. "I know what you

mean," he said. "I asked her what Ronda's favourite lunch was."

"And?" said Mandy.

James grinned. "Would you believe cornflakes?" he answered. "At least, I think that's what Libby said. She looked as if she was going to burst into tears so I didn't ask any more."

"I'm sure that Ronda is at the bottom of Libby's unhappiness," said Mandy.

"But if we can't ask Libby, how do we find out about Ronda? I've never heard of anybody called Ronda in Welford."

Mandy sighed. "Neither have I," she said. "And neither has Mum or Dad. I asked them."

James frowned. "What about your gran?" he said. "She knows everybody."

Mandy looked at James and smiled. "Brilliant!" she said. "If Gran doesn't know who Ronda is, then nobody does. Let's go round and see her after tea."

"I'll take Blackie," said James. "He loves going to Lilac Cottage."

Mandy giggled. "You mean he loves the fruit bushes!" she said.

James looked embarrassed. "Maybe I should leave him behind," he said.

"Oh, no, don't do that," said Mandy. "Gran and Grandad love Blackie."

"Get out of my raspberry canes, you young whippersnapper!" Grandad said, collaring Blackie.

James raised his eyebrows and looked at Mandy. But Mandy was laughing at Grandad and Blackie.

"Blackie knows you don't mean it," she said to her grandad.

Grandad grinned at her as Blackie put his front paws on his chest and started licking his face.

"Talk about soft," said Gran from the kitchen door. "Come on, Blackie, come and get a biscuit."

He gave a short bark and dashed into the kitchen after Gran.

"Cupboard love," said Grandad

brushing down his jumper. He looked at
Mandy and James. "How about a cool
drink?" he suggested.

Mandy and James nodded. "Grandad,
have you ever heard of a little girl called
Ronda?" Mandy asked.

"In Welford?" said Grandad.

Mandy shrugged. "I suppose she might
live on one of the farms up on the
moors," Mandy said.

"Maybe near where the Masters' farm
is," James added.

"The Masters?" said Gran as they came into the kitchen. "They have a free-range poultry farm up at Blackheath. How is little Libby getting on at school?"

Mandy frowned. "She seems really unhappy," she said, sitting down at the table.

Gran poured two glasses of orange juice for Mandy and James, and put a plate of home-made biscuits in front of them.

"We think it's got something to do with her friend, Ronda," said James.

"I don't think I know any Rondas," said Gran. "Where does she live?"

Mandy sighed. "We don't know," she said. "We thought if anybody would know, *you* would."

"Maybe Ronda is her sister," said Grandad.

Gran shook her head. "Libby is an only child," she said.

"Every time we ask Libby about Ronda she gets upset," said James. "If we knew what was upsetting her, maybe we could help."

Gran nodded. "I see," she said. "Of course it must be very lonely for Libby up on that farm. There isn't another house anywhere near it."

"So if she had a friend, it would be even more important to her," said Mandy.

"And if her friend was sick – or maybe moving away – then she would be really upset," said James.

"But you can't really begin to help until you know who Ronda is," said Grandad.

Mandy and James nodded.

"You leave it to me," Gran said. "I'll make enquiries."

"What do you know about this Ronda?" Grandad asked.

"Nothing much," said Mandy. "We know she wears a red coat . . ."

"And she likes cornflakes," said James.

Gran and Grandad looked at them blankly.

"Well!" said Gran. "That's *something* to go on, I suppose."

"How about asking Mrs McFarlane?" Grandad suggested. "She knows everybody."

Mr and Mrs McFarlane ran the post office in Welford. The post office was Mandy and James's favourite shop.

"Good idea," said James. "We'll pop in tomorrow on the way to school."

"And I'll start asking everyone at the WI," said Gran. She was chairwoman of Welford Women's Institute.

"Don't you worry," said Grandad. "We'll soon find out who this Ronda is!"

But by the end of the week, Ronda was still a mystery.

"Even Mrs McFarlane has never heard of her," Mandy said to her parents as she sat at the kitchen table, her homework spread out in front of her.

Mrs Hope pulled out a chair and sat down at the table beside Mandy. "You know," she said, "I've been thinking about this Ronda. Maybe she doesn't exist after all."

"But Libby talked about her. She's her friend," said Mandy.

Mrs Hope nodded sympathetically. "I know," she said. "But from what you've told me Libby seems to be quite lonely up on that farm. There aren't any other children about and she has no brothers and sisters."

Mr Hope frowned. "But what about Ronda?" he said, his dark eyes puzzled.

Mrs Hope pushed a curl of red hair back from her forehead, "Maybe there isn't any Ronda," she said. "Maybe she is an imaginary friend."

Mandy opened her mouth and looked at her mum. "Imaginary!" she said.

Emily Hope nodded. "Lonely children often have make-believe friends," she said. "Nobody else can see them, but they're very real to the child. And with Libby being an only child . . ."

"I'm an only child," said Mandy. "I

never had an imaginary friend."

Mr Hope smiled and his eyes twinkled. "Every patient that's passed through Animal Ark has been your friend, Mandy," he said. "You've never needed to make one up!"

Mandy grinned back. "I suppose so," she said. She thought for a moment. "So why does she get so upset when she talks about Ronda?" she asked.

Mrs Hope frowned. "I don't know. Maybe going to school has made her realise that Ronda isn't real. Maybe she doesn't want to let her pretend friend go."

Mandy thought hard. "I can see that," she said. "But I don't see how we can help Libby." She shook her head. "An imaginary friend. I never thought of that!"

3

Duchess in trouble

"That explains the red coat and eating cornflakes for lunch anyway," James said next day coming home from school. "I mean, imaginary friends don't have to act like real people."

"So what do we do?" asked Mandy.

James shrugged. "We can be Libby's

friends," he said. "At least until she gets over her shyness. Then she'll probably make friends with people in her own class."

"Maybe I could ask her to tea at Animal Ark," said Mandy.

"That's a good idea," James said. "You could show her some of the animals your mum and dad are looking after."

"I'll bet Libby would love to have a pet of her own," Mandy said. "What kind do you think she would like?"

As Mandy and James came into the reception at Animal Ark, Jean Knox looked up from her desk.

"Your mum is out on a call and your dad is in the operating room," she said.

Jean Knox was Animal Ark's receptionist. She sounded worried. Jean's glasses were dangling round her neck on their chain as usual, but her normally cheerful face looked strained.

"What's wrong, Jean?" Mandy said. "Is it an emergency?"

Jean nodded, her eyes serious. "It's Duchess," she said. "She got knocked down this afternoon."

Mandy and James looked at Jean in horror. "But Duchess is expecting her kittens any day now," Mandy said. "Is she badly hurt?"

"Her leg looked quite bad when Mrs Tanner brought her in," Jean said. "Your dad thought the shock might bring on the birth. So poor Duchess has got that to cope with too. Simon is in

there as well. They'll do everything they can."

Simon was the practice nurse – and a very good one.

"Does Richard know?" asked James.

"Mrs Tanner has gone home to tell him when he comes in from school," Jean said. "She said they'd be right back."

Mandy nodded. "Is there anything I can do, Jean?" she asked.

Jean looked out of the window behind her. "You could put the kettle on for a cup of tea, Mandy," she said. "That always helps. Oh, here come Richard and his mum now."

Mandy nodded and went into the kitchen to put the kettle on. James followed her.

"Poor Richard," he said. He unhooked some blue and white mugs from the kitchen dresser and put them on the worktop.

"Poor *Duchess*," Mandy said. "And

what's going to happen to her kittens?"

"Your dad will do his very best," James said reassuringly.

Mandy nodded. "I know that," she said. "Oh, I wish I knew what was happening in the operating room."

The kettle boiled. Mandy poured the water carefully into the teapot and set it on the tray.

"Come on," she said. "Let's go and keep Richard and his mum company while they're waiting."

Richard was sitting beside his mother in the reception area. He looked really pale and Mandy thought he was only just managing to hold back the tears.

"I'll never forgive myself," Mrs Tanner said to Jean. "I don't know how I managed to leave the door open. It was only for a minute."

Mandy put the teapot on a low table and James set down the tray.

"Tea," said Jean briskly as she came round the desk.

Mrs Tanner accepted a cup gratefully. Richard looked as if he hadn't even heard Jean.

"What hit Duchess?" James asked.

Mrs Tanner bit her lip. "A car," she said. "The driver was very apologetic but he said he expected Duchess to move faster than she did. He said he did his best to avoid her."

Mandy had a sudden vision of Duchess stalking across the road in her usual stately manner – except that, being pregnant with her kittens, she would be too heavy to make a dash for safety.

Richard just sat there, staring in front of him, his eyes dark with misery.

The operating-room door opened and they all turned towards it. Mandy could hear her heart beating as she forced herself to look at her dad's face.

"Richard," Mr Hope said softly.

Mandy could hardly breathe. Surely it wouldn't be bad news. Then she saw that her dad was smiling. He ran a hand through his thick hair and shook his head slightly.

"You've got quite a lady there," he said to Richard. "Duchess is now the proud mother of three kittens and, apart from her leg, I reckon she's going to be all right."

Mandy's heart was thumping so loudly she could hardly take in what her dad was saying. Duchess wasn't dead. Duchess was going to be all right. And three kittens!

"It's going to be a while before she's on her feet," Mr Hope continued. "And I'm afraid she might have a limp."

Richard's face brightened. "And her kittens," he said. "Are they OK?"

Mr Hope frowned. "We couldn't save two, I'm afraid, but the others look fine," he said. "Duchess is still pretty uncomfortable, so I think I'll keep her here until we see how she's managing."

"Can I see her?" Richard asked.

Mr Hope smiled. "Just for a moment,"

he said. "Simon is with her."

Richard disappeared into the operating room.

"Is she really going to be all right?" Mrs Tanner asked quietly.

Mr Hope nodded. "She'll need a lot of tender loving care for a while. Looking after the kittens might be difficult for her. But she should be as good as new in a couple of months' time – except for a bit of a limp."

"Oh, she'll get all the tender love and care we can give her," Mrs Tanner said.

"Now I'd better get her into the residential unit," Mr Hope said.

"Can we come?" said Mandy. "Can we see the kittens?"

"As if I could stop you!" said Mr Hope. "Come on then. But don't disturb her, she's very sleepy."

Richard turned as they came into the operating room. "Look!" he called quietly. "Look at Duchess and her kittens."

Mandy and James came to stand beside him. Simon was just finishing bandaging Duchess's leg. But Duchess wasn't paying too much attention to that. Instead she was licking the little bodies curled up against her, all her concentration on her kittens.

Mandy looked at the tiny, sightless little bundles of fur. "Oh, Duchess," she said. "They're beautiful."

"Well, well," said Mr Hope. "It looks as if Duchess is going to make a fine

mother." He scratched his head. "In fact, it just might be the best thing for her at the moment."

"What do you mean?" Mandy asked.

Mr Hope pointed to Duchess. "Look at her," he said. "She's so taken up with her kittens she doesn't seem to notice her leg is injured. I reckon she'll get better all the quicker with her little family to take her mind off her injuries."

Mandy smiled. "Of course she will," she said. "They're such beautiful babies!"

Mandy was so busy for the next few days, looking in on Duchess and the kittens and reporting back to Richard, that she almost forgot she had planned to ask Libby over for tea. It was only when her mum got a call from the Masters' farm that she remembered.

"Some of Mr Masters' hens are sick," Mrs Hope said as she put the phone down. "I'm going to take some vaccine up there. How would you like to come and see Libby, Mandy?"

"Could I?" said Mandy, turning away from Duchess. The kittens were getting stronger by the day.

"We can bring her back for tea if you like," Mrs Hope said. "I know you wanted to ask her."

Mandy blushed. "I forgot."

"Come on then," said Mrs Hope. "Get your wellies. If we're going to visit a poultry farm you'll need them."

The Masters' farm was high up on the moor. The whole of Welford was spread out below them as the Land-rover bumped its way along the farm track. Mandy looked up at the scudding clouds. The wind was fresh and strong, and the clouds made shadows on the hills. The Masters must get cut off in winter sometimes, she thought.

"I'm not surprised Libby invented a friend," Mandy said. "It must be lonely for her up here."

"It'll be nice for her to have a visitor

this afternoon," Mrs Hope said.

"There she is," said Mandy as they turned into the farmyard.

Libby was standing with her dad, waiting for Mrs Hope.

"Hi, Libby," said Mandy jumping down from the Land-rover as it stopped.

Libby's face broke into a pleased smile. "Mandy!" she said. She looked suddenly shy. "Would you like to see Ronda?"

Mandy's mouth dropped open in surprise. "See her?" she said.

Libby nodded.

Mandy looked at her mum. How on earth would she be able to "see" an imaginary friend? Maybe she would just have to pretend.

Mrs Hope looked just as surprised as Mandy felt.

"Oh, Ronda is a beauty," Mr Masters said. "You must see her. Come along."

Mandy and Mrs Hope watched as Mr Masters marched off across the farmyard with Libby skipping at his side.

"What do we do?" Mandy asked her mother.

Mrs Hope shrugged. "If Mr Masters can pretend to see Ronda, then so can we," she said. "Just do what he does."

Mandy and Mrs Hope rounded the corner of the barn and found Libby and her dad leaning over a wire enclosure.

"There she is," said Libby, looking in.

Mandy looked. There were about a dozen chickens in the enclosure and that was all. No little girl – no friend.

Libby opened a gate and made a chirruping sound. "Come on, Ronda," she said. "Come and meet Mandy."

Mandy looked in disbelief as a large hen with beautiful russet feathers strutted towards them. She marched through the gate and right up to Libby.

"Didn't I tell you she was a beauty?" Mr Masters said.

Libby looked at the hen proudly. "This is Ronda," she said to Mandy. "Isn't she

just beautiful? Look at her wonderful red feathers."

Mandy watched as the little girl put her hand in her pocket and brought out some corn.

"This is her favourite," Libby said. "Ronda just loves corn."

Ronda pecked up the corn. Then she stuck her head in Libby's pocket, looking for more.

"Ronda!" Libby giggled. "That tickles. Come and do your dance for Mandy."

Libby stood up and let a stream of corn fall from her hand. Ronda picked her way delicately amongst it, pecking it up, following the trail as the little girl made circles of corn on the ground.

Mandy looked at Ronda. The red coat. The corn. That was the mystery explained. Ronda was a hen. And not just an ordinary hen — a dancing one!

4

The amazing dancing hen

"You should put her on the stage," said Mandy. "She's terrific!"

"She's a Rhode Island Red," Libby said proudly, scattering the rest of the corn for Ronda.

"She's more like a member of the family than a hen," said Mr Masters. He laughed.

"Sometimes she comes into the house to watch TV. She just settles herself down beside Libby. You'd think she understood every word."

Mrs Hope smiled. "Rhode Island Reds make great pets," she said. "They often get really attached to a family."

Mr Masters scratched his head. "Ronda is certainly attached to Libby," he said. "When she was ill Ronda used to come and sit beside her. She was great company for her."

"She follows me around everywhere," said Libby. Then her face fell. "Only she hates me going to school. She misses me — and I miss her."

"Maybe you could have a look at Ronda while you're here, Mrs Hope," Mr Masters said. "She doesn't seem to be ill, but I don't mind telling you I've been quite worried about her recently. She hasn't been laying well at all and I don't think her coat is as healthy as it should be."

Mrs Hope bent down and gathered Ronda gently into her hands, turning the hen round and examining her.

"Her feathers *are* a bit dull," said Mrs Hope. "Nothing to worry about yet. Is she eating?"

Libby shook her head. "Sometimes she doesn't eat at all when I'm not here."

"That could be serious," said Mrs Hope. "If she doesn't eat properly she'll stop laying altogether." She looked at Libby. "I think Ronda is pining for you,"

she said. "Missing you while you're at school."

"Does that mean she'll get sick?" Libby asked.

Mrs Hope smiled reassuringly, but she looked concerned. "Maybe," she said. "So what we have to do is find some way of stopping her pining and that will stop her getting sick."

"How?" said Libby. "Mummy says I have to go to school – and I can't take Ronda."

"No," said Mrs Hope. "It's a problem, Libby."

Mandy looked at her mother. What on earth could they do? Libby was unhappy because she had to leave Ronda at home. Ronda was pining because she missed Libby. If Ronda got sick, Libby would be even more unhappy.

"Is there anything you can do for her at the moment?" Mr Masters asked Mrs Hope.

Mrs Hope looked thoughtful. "I can

give you some vitamin supplements to put in her feed," she said. "It would probably be a good idea to make sure she got some extra protein as well. But what she really needs is something to fill the gap that Libby leaves when she goes to school."

"You mean, like something to interest her," said Mandy.

"Something to stop her missing Libby," said Mr Masters. He looked at Mandy and Libby. "That *is* a puzzle," he said. "I'll have to think about that . . . but meanwhile I should see to my other hens."

Mandy and Libby watched as Mrs Hope and Mr Masters made their way across the farmyard to the henhouses.

"If Ronda stops eating, she'll die," Libby said to Mandy.

Mandy put out a hand and stroked the hen's coat gently. Ronda ruffled her feathers and settled close to Libby's chest.

"We won't let that happen, Libby,"

Mandy said. "We'll think of something."

Libby looked at Mandy. "Promise?"

Mandy looked at the little girl with her hen cradled in her arms. "I promise."

Mandy was very quiet all the way home.

"You're worrying about Ronda, aren't you?" her mum said as they turned into the driveway at Animal Ark.

Mandy nodded. "I didn't know hens could get so attached to somebody," she said.

Mrs Hope smiled. "It isn't just dogs and cats that get fond of people," she said. "All kinds of animals miss their owners and start to mope. Rhode Island Reds are famous for becoming part of the family."

Mandy bit her lip. "I promised Libby I would think of something," she said.

"Meantime you've got to say goodbye to your favourite patients," Mrs Hope said, getting out of the Land-rover. "Richard and his mother are coming to collect Duchess and the kittens tonight."

Mandy smiled. "I won't mind really," she said. "Duchess will be much happier at home with Richard."

"Even though she has been in the best animal hotel in Welford," Mrs Hope said.

Mandy grinned. "The very best!"

Mr Hope gave Duchess and the kittens a final check before Richard took them home.

Mandy cuddled the Persian cat gently. "No more running out of the door, Duchess," she said, trying to sound severe. "You're a grown-up mum now. You've got to give a good example to your kittens."

Duchess just yawned.

"I don't think Duchess will be running around much for a while," said James. "She'll be far too busy looking after her babies. She won't want to let them out of her sight."

James and Mandy watched as Richard

walked off down the path. He had the kittens safely tucked up in a carrying basket, while his mother carried Duchess in a separate box.

"That reminds me," said Mandy. "I've found out who Ronda is."

James listened open-mouthed while Mandy told him all about the hen.

"Poor Libby," James said when Mandy had finished. "It must be rotten for her going off to school every day, knowing that Ronda will be pining."

"What Ronda needs is something to hold her attention," Mandy said. "Something to stop her missing Libby."

James thought for a moment. "Chicks!" he said.

"What?" said Mandy.

James turned to her, his eyes gleaming with excitement. "Chicks," he said again. "If Ronda had chicks to look after, she wouldn't have time to miss Libby. Look at Duchess and her kittens! She hardly even notices her sore leg."

Mandy looked at him in delight. "James, you're brilliant!" she said. Then her face fell. "No, that won't work."

"Why not?" asked James.

Mandy shook her head. "For chicks you need eggs," she replied. "And Mr Masters is afraid that Ronda is going to stop laying,"

"Oh," said James. "That *is* a problem."

Mandy looked at him. "Let's go and ask Dad," she said. "There must be something we can do. It's *such* a good idea, James."

"They don't have to be Ronda's eggs," said Mr Hope. "Just as long as the eggs are fertile, Ronda can sit on them and hatch out chicks. Then the chicks will belong to Ronda."

"What do you mean, fertile?" asked Mandy.

"Some eggs will hatch into chicks – they're the fertile ones," Mr Hope explained. "Others don't hatch into chicks. They're called infertile. They're the eggs we eat for breakfast."

Mandy and James looked at each other in delight.

"There's only one problem," Mrs Hope said.

Mandy and James looked at her.

"Ronda wasn't broody when I saw her," she said.

"What does *that* mean?" James asked.

Mrs Hope smiled. "If a hen is going to hatch out eggs it has to be broody," she said. "That means it has to want to sit on its nest. Hatching eggs takes a long time – three whole weeks. You can't force a hen to sit on eggs."

"So it won't work," said Mandy.

"I wouldn't say that," Mr Hope said. "There are ways of encouraging a hen to turn broody, and Rhode Island Reds make very good broodies."

"What sorts of ways?" asked Mandy.

"Like putting china eggs in its nest," said Mr Hope. "You can sometimes persuade a hen to sit on china eggs, then replace them with real ones once the hen has decided to sit on them."

"But how would we persuade Ronda to sit on the china eggs?" Mandy said.

"Ah, that might take a bit of patience," said Mr Hope.

"And a bit of luck," added Mrs Hope.

Mandy and James looked at each other. Mandy lifted her chin. "It's worth a try," she said.

James grinned at her.

"Uh-oh," he said. "I know that look! Poor Ronda doesn't stand a chance. She'll be sitting on her eggs in no time at all."

5

A difficult task

"So what we've got to do is try to make Ronda want to sit on her nest," Mandy said to Libby next day at school.

"Do you think your dad has any china eggs?" James asked.

Libby nodded. "Oh, yes," she said. "I've seen what he does with them."

"Does it really work?" said Mandy.

Libby frowned. "Yes," she said. "But he only ever does it with hens that have already started sitting on their nest."

"You mean they've *gone* broody," said James.

Libby nodded again. "I don't see how we can get Ronda to do that," the little girl said. "She always wants to follow me around."

"Then you'll just have to sit on the nest with her," James joked.

Libby looked at him in surprise and smiled. "I never thought of that," she said.

"James was joking," Mandy said.

Libby giggled. "I know," she said. "I'd be a bit big for a nest!"

Mandy and James laughed.

"Why don't we come up to the farm tomorrow," Mandy suggested. "I know Dad is coming up to see if the vaccine worked."

Libby nodded. "That would be great!

And I'll ask Dad about the china eggs."

"I don't know about this," Mr Masters said next day. "Libby has made a special nest for Ronda in the broody pen by the barn. There are a few broodies there already, but Ronda doesn't look as if she wants to sit on the nest."

"Let's go and see if we can help," Mandy said to James.

"Good luck!" Mr Hope said as he and Mr Masters went off towards the big hen pen.

Mandy and James found Libby trying to coax Ronda on to her nesting-box. Ronda strutted around the scratching area.

"Come on, Ronda," Libby said softly. She looked round as Mandy and James appeared. Then she put her fingers to her lips. "Shh," she said. "We have to be quiet or we'll disturb the other nesting birds."

Mandy looked in the nesting-box. It

was tucked neatly under the low roof of the pen and lined with straw.

"Why is it up there?" whispered James.

"The nesting-box has to be off the ground," said Libby. "It's to keep the eggs safe from any rats or foxes that might get into the pen."

Poor Libby didn't look very happy. "Dad says if Ronda doesn't start to sit soon she'll have to come out of the broody pen," she said. "He thinks she'll put the other broodies off. All their chicks are due next week."

Mandy looked along the length of the pen. There were flutterings from all the other nesting-boxes and the soft sound of hens clucking to themselves in the warm darkness of the nests. It was very peaceful.

"Do they stay there all the time?" James said.

Libby nodded. "They come out for a scratch-around every day," she said. "But only for about fifteen minutes. The eggs would get cold if the hens left the nest for longer than that."

"How long do they stay there?" asked Mandy.

"Three weeks," Libby said. She smiled. "Can you imagine sitting in the same place for three weeks? No wonder Ronda doesn't want to do it."

Mandy looked at the Rhode Island Red. "But it's natural for hens to sit on their eggs," she said.

"I know she would just love chicks," Libby said. "She'd make a wonderful mother."

"Have you tried lifting her on to the nest?" James wondered.

Libby nodded. "But I'll try again," she said. "You never know."

Mandy and James watched as Libby carefully slid her hands under Ronda's body and lifted the hen into her arms. Ronda ruffled her feathers and settled down in the little girl's arms. Libby carried her over to the nest and placed her there.

Ronda settled down and began to peck at the straw in the nest, making soft burbling noises.

Mandy and James stood watching silently. Ronda fluttered again and settled deeper into the straw.

Libby rose and Ronda looked round sharply, ready to move and follow her mistress.

"Maybe if you stayed with her for a little while," Mandy suggested.

Libby looked at Ronda. "When I put her on before she just got off again," she said. "Do you think she'll stay this time?"

"She might," said Mandy. "If she gets really comfortable."

"I'll stay with her for a while," Libby said. "Can you and James get the china eggs from Mum? Then we'll be ready if she decides to sit."

Mandy and James slipped quietly out of the broody pen. They didn't want to alarm Ronda. Mandy looked back: Ronda was sitting quietly on the nest and

Libby was standing beside her in the darkness. Just as she turned to go Mandy heard Ronda make a low, contented clucking sound. Maybe their plan was going to work after all.

Mr Hope came out of the farmhouse with Mr and Mrs Masters. He was ready to go, but Mandy and James were really reluctant to leave just yet. Mrs Masters had two big brown eggs in her hand.

"These are for you," she said to Mandy and James.

They looked at them with interest. Then Mandy realised what they were.

"They're the china eggs," she said. "But they look just like real ones."

Mr Masters chuckled. "That's the idea," he said. "They have to be good if they're going to fool a hen."

"How is it going down there?" Mrs Masters asked.

Mandy and James looked at each other.

"Ronda was sitting on the nest when we left," said Mandy.

"Libby is with her," James added.

Mr Masters shook his head. "You have to be sure she's going to sit tight before you put any fertile eggs under her," he said.

"How long before you could be sure?" James asked.

Mr Masters scratched his chin. "If she's still there in the morning, we might risk it at dusk tomorrow," he said.

"Why dusk?" said Mandy.

Mr Hope smiled at her. "Think," he said. "What do hens do at night?"

"Go to sleep?" said James.

"They roost," said Mandy. "They go to sleep on perches up off the ground so the foxes and rats can't harm them."

Mr Hope nodded. "Hens always roost at night," he said. "So if Ronda is going to come off the nest she'll come off at dusk when it's time to roost. If she stays on the nest the chances are she's broody. You could try her with the china eggs tonight if you're careful how you put them in."

"Can we stay and do that?" asked Mandy. "Do we have to go now?"

"I'll tell you what," Mr Hope said. "I've got a few more calls to make. What if I collect you on my way home?"

"That would be great, Dad," Mandy said. "Thanks a lot."

"Do you think it'll work?" James asked.

Mr Masters shrugged. "It might," he said. "Some breeds make better broodies than others and Rhode Island Reds are usually pretty good. Just don't go giving Ronda a fright. You'll have to be very quiet down there."

"I'll pick you up later," Mr Hope said. "Be good."

Mandy and James waved goodbye to Mr Hope and ran down to the broody pen with the china eggs.

Mandy held her breath. Maybe Ronda was strutting around the scratching area again. But there was no sign of the Rhode Island Red as she and James rounded the corner of the barn.

"Shh," said James.

They peered into the pen. Libby was still there — and Ronda was still sitting on her nest.

Mandy hardly dared to breathe. Maybe it would work. The china eggs were warm in her hands. All they had to do now was make sure nothing disturbed Ronda before dusk. It would be agony waiting but it had to be done.

The sun had gone behind the barn and Mandy could hear the hens on the other nesting-boxes settling down for the night. There were faint rustlings and murmurings. Mandy and James sat quietly at the front of the pen. Libby was still in there with Ronda. The light was fading from the sky. Now was the moment. If Ronda went to roost, they had failed. Another half-hour or so and they would know.

"I'm hungry," James whispered. "Tea seems a long time ago."

"Just a while longer," Mandy whispered back.

There was a movement behind them and Libby appeared. Her eyes were shining.

"I think she's settled," she said. "She's been sitting on the same spot for ages. Should we try the eggs?"

Mandy and James looked at each other and nodded.

"*You'd* better do it," said Mandy to Libby. "You won't scare her."

"But I've never done it before," Libby said.

"You must've seen your dad do it," said James.

"Just slide them under her," Mandy said. "They're warm already. It's just to get her used to sitting on eggs."

Libby bit her lip. "OK, I'll try," she said.

She slipped back into the broody pen. Mandy and James heard her speaking softly to Ronda, soothing her, calming her. Mandy peered into the darkness. She saw Libby slip an egg under the hen's body. Ronda stirred and fluttered. Then she seemed to settle deeper into the nest. Libby turned to look at James and Mandy.

"Now the other one," Mandy whispered.

Libby took the other egg out of her pocket and very, very gently slipped it under Ronda. This time the hen barely stirred. Libby waited a moment then

slipped quietly out of the hen pen.

None of them spoke until they were right outside the pen. They stopped by the barn and looked back.

"Well done, Libby," Mandy said. "That was perfect."

"You didn't disturb her at all," James said.

Libby flushed with pleasure but her eyes were worried. "I hope she stays on the nest," she said.

Mandy and James nodded. "All we can do now is wait," Mandy said. "If she's still there in the morning the chances are she'll sit."

Libby looked at her. "The morning?" she said. "It's such a long time to wait."

"Just think of all the chicks Ronda is going to have," Mandy said. "That's worth waiting for, isn't it?"

Libby's eyes shone. "Oh, yes," she said. "That *is* worth waiting for!"

6

Success!

Mandy and James saw Libby in the playground first thing next morning. She was in the middle of a group of her classmates, all talking at once and asking her questions.

"She's still there," Libby said, running up to them. "Ronda is still on the nest."

"Libby is going to let us all see the chicks when they're hatched," said a little girl with bright-red hair.

"And you can come up to the farm and visit them, Nikki," Libby said.

"What about the rest of us?" said a dark-haired boy.

"You can all come, Tim," Libby said, looking round the little group. "All of you."

Mandy smiled. Libby had quite made up her mind that Ronda was going to have a whole brood of chicks.

"That's great," Mandy said. "But we've only put the *china* eggs in so far."

"When can we try real eggs?" James wanted to know.

Libby's face was glowing with excitement.

"Dad says we can try tonight," she said. "He thinks we should wait till dusk again, when she's settled for the night. That's the best time to try. You *will* be able to come, won't you? Mum said she would come and fetch you both after tea and take you home again later."

"Of course we'll come," said Mandy.

"Just you try and stop us!" James added.

The bell went and Libby dashed off with her friends.

"Libby is getting on really well with the rest of her class now," Mandy said.

James nodded. "Look at her!" he said. "She's got loads of friends."

Mandy smiled. "It looks like Libby's problem is solved," she said. "Now all we have to do is make sure Ronda has a brood of chicks to keep her company."

"Now all these eggs have a good chance of being fertile," Mr Masters said.

Mandy, James and Libby peered into the basket he was holding. Seven brown eggs nestled amongst the straw.

"Does that mean they'll turn into chicks?" Libby asked.

Mr Masters nodded. "If we're really lucky," he said. "We'll test them once

Ronda has been sitting on them for a little while, so don't be disappointed if one or two aren't fertile."

Libby looked at the eggs. "Just think," she said. "In three weeks' time they're all going to be chickens."

Mr Masters laughed. "In three weeks' time, if they all hatch out, they're going to be a lot of *work*. A real chick challenge. I hope you realise that!"

"Oh, we'll help," said Mandy.

"That's right," James said. "We know that young animals are always a lot of work. We don't mind."

Mr Masters raised his eyebrows. "I certainly hope so," he said. "It's going to keep Ronda busy, too."

"Ronda will love it," Libby said firmly. "I just know she will."

Mr Masters laughed again. "OK, then," he said. "Let's get started. First we'll get Ronda off the nest. Then we'll get the real eggs on it."

"But how do we do that?" asked Libby.

Mr Masters smiled. "She needs one good feed a day and a scratch-around," he said. "We can replace the eggs while she's feeding and with any luck she'll accept them."

Libby carried the tin dish of maize and corn carefully into the pen and put it down. Mandy fetched some water.

"Grain is the best feed for a sitting hen," Mr Masters said. "If you give her soft food, the droppings can foul the eggs."

"Couldn't you wash them?" James said.

Mr Masters shook his head. "Once she starts incubating the eggs you don't want to touch them any more than you have to," he said. "They can get cold very quickly and then they won't hatch out."

Libby tapped the side of the feed dish and there was a fluttering sound as Ronda flew down from the nest. She made for the food right away.

"OK, while she's busy with that you'd better get on with changing the eggs," Mr Masters said.

Mandy, Libby and James slipped into the pen and reached up to the nesting-box. Mandy scooped out the china eggs while James and Libby filled the nest with the real ones.

When they came back out Ronda was having a good long drink of water. They watched as she lifted her head and strutted over to a corner of the pen.

"What is she doing now?" asked Mandy.

"She's going to have a bath," Libby said. "She loves baths."

"What's she going to bath in?" asked James.

Libby giggled. "In the dust," she said. "Chickens always take dust-baths. It keeps their feathers clean."

James shook his head. "I wonder what Mum would say if *I* tried that," he said.

Mandy grinned. "She must be used to it," she said. "Blackie is always rolling in the dust."

Libby turned towards them. "Where

is Blackie?" she said. "You never bring him with you."

"We thought he might upset Ronda and the other chickens," James explained. "We wouldn't want to scare them."

Mr Masters nodded. "That's good thinking," he said. "It's easy for a hen to be scared off the nest, even by the friend-liest of dogs."

Libby's mouth drooped. Then she cheered up. "Just wait till Ronda has her chicks," she said. "You can bring Blackie then. I'll bet he'll love them."

"Now," said Mr Masters, "let's see if Ronda will go back on the nest – and accept those eggs."

Mandy, Libby and James held their breath as Mr Masters picked Ronda up gently and put her back on her nest. Ronda ruffled her feathers and shifted her weight. Mr Masters came and stood beside the others.

"Just keep very still and watch," he said. Ronda bent and poked at the nest with her beak, shifting bits of straw, burrowing her feet and body into it, ruffling her feathers. Then she gave one last wriggle and settled down – and stayed absolutely still.

Mr Masters let out a low whistle and Mandy looked at him. "Well, I have to hand it to you," he said. "It looks as if you've done it. It looks as if Ronda's going to hatch those eggs after all."

The children looked at one another.

"I knew we could do it," Libby said,

her eyes shining. "I just *knew* it."

The sun had set now and the yard was deep in shadow. From all along the pen came the sounds of birds settling down for the night.

"Now we must leave her to get on with it," said Mr Masters. "It's up to Ronda now."

"But we have to look after her," Libby said.

"Indeed you do," said Mr Masters. "I've made out a list of all the things you have to do for your chick challenge. Come and have a look."

Mandy, James and Libby followed him into the house.

"There's your list," Mrs Masters said as she poured out juice for them and put a huge sponge cake on the kitchen table.

"Wow!" said James. "That cake looks brilliant."

"Help yourself." Mrs Masters smiled.

Mandy picked up the list and sat down at the table. "Look at this," she said. "We have to make sure Ronda gets plenty of grit to help her digest her food."

"That's important," said Mr Masters. "Hens don't have teeth and grit helps to grind their food up."

"And protein," said James, through a mouthful of cake.

Mr Masters nodded. "It might not seem like it, but it's hard work sitting on a nest for three weeks," he added. "She'll only be out for feeding and exercise once a day so it'll need to be a good feed."

"And what about afterwards, once the chicks are hatched?" Mandy asked.

"That's when the real work starts," Mr Masters said, smiling. "You won't get much peace then."

"Where are Ronda and her chicks going to live?" Libby asked.

"They could go into the coops with the other hens and chicks," said her mother.

Libby put her head on one side. "Wouldn't it be nice if Ronda had a little house of her own?" she asked.

Mr Masters ran a hand through his hair. "I'm sorry, Libby," he said. "I just don't have time at the moment for building a new coop."

Mandy looked up. "I know somebody who would do it," she said. "And we could help him."

"Who?" said Libby.

Mandy grinned. "Grandad," she said. "He made a rabbit hutch for Jack Gardiner. I'm sure he could make a hen coop."

"That would be brilliant," Libby said. "When can we ask him?"

"Are you sure he wouldn't mind?" Mrs Masters asked Mandy.

James laughed. "He won't," he said. "Mandy's grandad is used to it – so is her gran. They're great at helping out."

"That *would* be kind," said Mr Masters. "But you mustn't put your grandad to too much trouble, Mandy."

"He'd love to make a special house just

for Ronda and her family," Mandy said.

"A special house for a special hen," said James.

Libby nibbled on a large slice of sponge cake. "Isn't it lovely? Ronda is going to have a whole family of chicks!"

7

A house for Ronda

"And you'll help us, Grandad?" Mandy said.

Grandad looked at Mandy, Libby and James.

"As if I had any choice!" he said with a twinkle in his eye. "Of course I'll help you. But I'll need a picture of a hen coop.

I'm not sure I know what's needed."

"Oh, that's all right," Mandy said. "I've brought a book."

"And Dad made some drawings," Libby added.

Gran laughed out loud. "It's nice to see that you came prepared. While you're looking at that book, I'll put the kettle on."

"Good idea," said Grandad. He was already studying the drawing Libby had brought.

By the time Gran had brought the tea out into the garden, Grandad was making a list.

"We'll get the wood from Fenton's timberyard," he said. "And we'll need some chicken wire. I think I've got some roofing felt in the garage already."

"When can we start?" Mandy asked as Gran handed round tea.

Grandad took a mug of tea and dived into the biscuit barrel. "Mmm," he said. "Ginger biscuits. My favourite."

"Grandad!" Mandy said.

"Tomorrow is Saturday," he said. "Be here bright and early and we'll start then."

"We'll be here," said James.

"And I'll get my dad to bring me," said Libby.

"Just look how much we've done in two days," James said on Sunday afternoon.

Mandy pushed her fair hair out of her eyes and looked at their handiwork. The coop was just like a little wooden house. The roof was covered in roofing felt. There was a small opening at one side and a sliding door at the other.

"We've still to do the run," Grandad said.

James smiled. "When it's finished it'll look just like a tiny house with a front garden," he said.

"It looks terrific," Libby said. "Ronda is going to be so pleased."

"How is she?" Mandy asked.

"Dad says she's doing really well,"

Libby answered. "He's going to test the eggs this week. Do you want to come and see?"

"Sure," said James. "When is he going to do it?"

"Thursday, I think," Libby said. "He has to do it while Ronda is out for her exercise."

"I reckon this coop should be finished by Thursday," Grandad said. "Why don't I take you up to the farm and we can deliver it then?"

"Brilliant," said Mandy. "Can we start on the run?"

Grandad laughed. "All right. Just let me finish my tea break!"

It was quite late when they finished fitting the frame of the run together and tacked on the chicken wire. The run *was* like a little garden in front of the coop, as James said – a place for Ronda and her chicks to scratch about in and get some exercise.

"Just the top to do now," said Grandad.

"Top?" said James.

Grandad nodded. "You have to put a mesh lid on top of the run to keep out vermin like rats and foxes," he said.

"Are we going to do that now?" asked Mandy.

Grandad shook his head. "It's too late," he said. "But I'll have it done by Thursday, don't you worry." He looked at the coop. "I could never have got on this fast without you three."

Mandy, James and Libby grinned at one another.

"It was great fun," said Libby. Her eyes lit up. "Do you think we could paint it once we get it to the farm?"

"That's a brilliant idea," said Mandy. "What colour?"

Libby thought for a moment. Then she giggled. "Red, of course," she said. "Because Ronda is a Rhode Island Red."

Mr and Mrs Masters thought the coop was terrific too.

"I should get you to come up and make a few more of those for me," Mr Masters joked, as he and Grandad stood looking down at it. "It was really good of you to take the time to do it."

"It was a pleasure," Grandad said. "Now, where is this famous Ronda that I've heard so much about?"

Mr Masters led the way to the broody pen.

"There she is," Libby whispered.

"Time for her daily feed and exercise," Mr Masters said.

Mandy, James and Libby fetched the food and water, but Ronda didn't seem to want to move.

"Rhode Island Reds are such good broodies," Mr Masters said. "Sometimes it's hard to get them off the nest once they've decided to sit."

Libby went very softly up to Ronda and lifted her down from the nest. "There," she said. "Have your dinner and your drink."

"And don't forget your bath, Ronda," James added.

Mandy looked at Mr Masters. He had a torch in one hand.

"I'm going to candle the eggs now," he said to her.

Mandy looked puzzled. "Candle?" she repeated.

"Watch," Mr Masters said.

Libby, Mandy, James and Grandad all gathered round. It was getting quite dark now.

Mr Masters picked an egg out of the nest and held it between his thumb and forefinger. "Gather closer," he said. "We want to cut out all the light we can."

They moved closer together, hardly breathing as Mr Masters switched on the powerful torch and held it behind the egg.

"Look," he said. "This one is fertile."

Mandy looked, but all she could see was a big dark patch inside the egg and a small clear area at the thick end of the shell.

"What's that dark patch?" she asked.

Mr Masters switched off the light. "That's the chicken," he said, smiling.

"What?" said Mandy in amazement. "Can we see it again?"

Mr Masters put the egg back and picked up another. Again he switched on the torch and Mandy looked carefully. There, inside the eggshell, was the dark patch which would develop into a chicken.

"That's incredible," said James as

Mr Masters replaced that egg and took another.

This time the torchlight shone clear through the shell.

"What does that mean?" Mandy asked.

"I'm afraid there's no chicken inside that one," Mr Masters said. "It's infertile."

"Oh, what a pity," Libby said.

Mandy leaned over, eager to see if there was a chicken inside the next one. "Why did you say you were going to 'candle' them?" she asked.

Mr Masters smiled. "Because before torches were invented farmers had to do this with a candle," he said.

"Oh, right," said Mandy. "That one has a chicken inside."

"Would you like to try it?" Mr Masters asked.

Mandy looked at him in the torchlight. "May I?"

"Of course," Mr Masters replied. "Go ahead, pick up an egg."

Mandy reached into the nest and lifted

out a brown egg. "Oh," she said. "I'd forgotten they would be warm."

"Now hold it carefully," Mr Masters said. "I'll shine the torch for you."

Mandy held the egg between her thumb and forefinger, as he had done.

"Not too tightly," Mr Masters said. Then he switched on the light.

Mandy looked at the egg. "Fertile," she said happily. "Just think. I'm holding a tiny little chicken inside an egg. It's wonderful!"

Mr Masters swivelled the torch round so that it was pointing at the nest and Mandy replaced the egg. There were two more eggs: one fertile, one infertile.

"That's pretty good," Mr Masters said. "Five out of seven is a very good average."

"Five chicks," said Libby. "Oh, I can hardly wait another whole week!"

"Time to get Ronda back on the nest, I think," Mr Masters said. "We don't want these eggs getting cold."

Libby carried Ronda in and she settled back happily on her nest.

"Will she notice that two eggs are missing?" Libby asked.

Mr Masters shook his head. "I don't think so," he said.

"That's good," said Libby. "Everybody at school is going to be so excited. Five chicks! I just can't wait to tell them!"

8

Eggs in danger

Mr Hope took Mandy and James up to Blackheath Farm the following weekend to paint the coop.

"I'm going to put a notice on the bulletin board at school every day," Libby said. "Everybody wants to know about Ronda and the chick challenge —

especially now there are only a few days to go."

James dipped his brush in the pot of red paint. "I think that's a great idea," he said.

Mandy smiled. Libby was making lots of friends now that all her classmates were interested in Ronda.

"How are Nikki and Tim?" she asked.

"They want to adopt a chick each once they're hatched," Libby said.

"Do they want to keep them as pets?" Mandy asked.

Libby shook her head. "Oh, no," she said. "I wouldn't want Ronda to lose any of her chicks. But Tim and Nikki can come here and see them every week. The chicks will be their special ones. They're already thinking up names for them."

"What about the rest of the chicks?" said James.

Libby put her head on one side. "Laura and Jack would like to adopt one as well," she said. "And Susan Davis. In fact everybody would like a special chick."

"You won't have enough to go round," said Mandy.

"Oh, that's all right," Libby said. "Ronda is sure to have more chicks – enough for everybody."

Mandy laughed. "Ronda *is* going to be busy. It's lucky she's got such a nice coop."

James looked at the coop. "You know, it looks so good it should have a name. Just like a proper house," he said.

"What? Like Blackheath Farm?" said Libby.

"Or Animal Ark?" added Mandy.

James nodded and his face lit up.

"That's what we need," he said. "A sign – like the Animal Ark sign."

"With the name on it," said Libby.

"But what would you call it?" said Mandy.

"How about Chicken Cottage," James suggested.

"Or Hen House," added Libby.

"I know," Mandy said. "Ronda's Residence."

"What does 'residence' mean?" Libby asked.

"It's a posh name for a house," James explained.

Libby giggled. "That's OK then," she said. "Ronda is posh, too."

"So what we need is a post and a board," Mandy said.

"Dad is sure to have some wood somewhere," Libby said. "Let's go and ask him."

They found Mr Masters mending a fence in the farmyard near the broody pen. Ronda was the only broody left now. All the other hens had hatched their chicks.

"I've got just what you need," he said. "Come on. I'll cut it to the right size for you."

They followed Mr Masters into the barn and watched while he got the wood out of the store and measured it. Then he cut it, smoothed the edges and gave it to them.

"You paint it and then I'll put it up for you," he said. "And remember: nice neat lettering." He picked up a wooden pole. "This should do for a post," he added.

"How do you spell 'residence'?" Libby asked.

Mandy grinned. "Maybe we'll just call it Ronda's Range," she said. "After all, she is a free-range chicken."

"That's a good idea," said Libby. "Ronda's Range!"

Suddenly there was a commotion outside. Libby turned, her face anxious. "That's Ronda!" she said. "Something's happened."

Before anybody could stop her, Libby was out of the door and racing towards the broody pen.

Mr Masters was right behind her, still carrying the pole. Mandy and James followed. They rounded the corner of the barn and stopped dead in their tracks.

"Go away! Go away!" Libby was yelling.

The Rhode Island Red was running round in front of the broody pen, squawking and flapping her wings.

Then Mandy saw what Libby was shouting at. It was a fox. Mr Masters scooped Libby up with one hand and thrust her behind him.

"Hold on to her," he said to Mandy, "and stay back. A cornered fox is dangerous."

Mandy hugged Libby and held on tight. Libby wriggled in her grasp. "The fox. It'll get Ronda! It'll get the eggs!" she cried, tears streaming down her face.

"No it won't," said James. "Look!"

Libby looked up. Mr Masters walked towards the fox and threw the wooden post. Mandy gasped, then she saw that he hadn't thrown the pole to hurt the fox, but just to frighten it. The fox jumped sideways and, quick as a flash, streaked through the hole in the fence

and out into the open fields beyond.

"It's all right now. It's gone," Mandy said to Libby.

But Libby was still crying. "Ronda!" she cried and ran towards her. But Ronda was too upset. She continued to run around, flapping her wings.

"Leave her for a moment," Mr Masters said. "Give her time to calm down."

But Ronda didn't calm down. She wouldn't even let Libby pick her up at first and when she eventually did she certainly wouldn't let the little girl put her back on the nest. She wriggled and fluttered and wouldn't settle.

"The eggs," Mandy said. "What are we going to do about the eggs?"

Mr Masters looked at his watch. "We'll have to do something soon," he said. "If we leave it much longer the eggs will get cold."

"And then they won't hatch," added Libby. "Oh, that bad fox."

Mandy gave her a hug. "It wasn't the fox's fault," she said. "That's the way they're made. It's just their nature."

"It's my fault," Mr Masters said. "If I'd mended that fence the fox wouldn't have got in."

"But you were helping us instead," said James.

Mr Masters smiled. "OK," he said. "It's nobody's fault. But we still have a problem to solve. Come on, I need your help."

Mandy and James followed Mr Masters

into the hay barn while Libby tried to calm Ronda. Mr Masters picked up a wooden box and pointed to a pile of hay.

"You two fill the box," he said. "I'll go and get the eggs."

Mandy and James didn't ask any questions. Mr Masters was obviously in a hurry. He was back in no time, with Ronda's eggs carefully laid on straw on the bottom of a basket.

"Now, if you can make a hollow in that hay," he said, "I'll put the eggs in."

Mandy scooped out a handful of hay and pressed the rest down.

"Is this to keep the eggs warm?" James asked.

Mr Masters nodded. "It's called a haybox," he said. "Farmers used to use them all the time before they had incubators. The hay keeps the eggs warm."

"I've heard of hayboxes," said Mandy. "But I thought they were for cooking."

Mr Masters smiled. "In the old days people used them for cooking too," he said. "If you put a hot casserole in here it would keep on cooking for hours."

"It won't cook the eggs, though, will it?" said James, alarmed.

Mr Masters shook his head. "No," he said. "It only *preserves* the heat. It'll just keep the eggs nicely warm."

He lifted the eggs very gently out of the basket and placed them carefully in amongst the hay.

"We can't keep them in here too long," he said. "But if we can keep them warm enough and get Ronda back on to the nest, we might have a chance."

Mandy covered the eggs over with more hay. "How long have we got?" she asked.

Mr Masters shrugged. "I wouldn't like to risk more than a few hours," he said. "I've heard of people keeping eggs warm a lot longer than that, but it's a big risk."

Mandy bit her lip. "Libby will calm Ronda down," she said. "You'll see."

Mr Masters packed more hay into the

box and put it safely up on a shelf in the barn.

"Come on," he said. "Let's see how she's getting on."

Libby was sitting in the dust with Ronda beside her. The Rhode Island Red was a lot calmer; she wasn't running around any more. But she was pecking nervously at the grass and scratching in the dirt.

"She won't go back," Libby said softly.

Mr Masters kept his voice low. "Give her time," he said. "Don't rush her."

It was the hardest thing. Mandy wanted to lift Ronda up and put her back on the nest but she knew that would be the wrong thing to do. It would be even worse if Ronda started to sit on her eggs and then got off the nest again.

Libby sat in the dirt beside Ronda, singing to her in a low voice. The hen began to scratch at the dirt less and less, and moved closer to the little girl. Libby reached out a hand and smoothed Ronda's ruffled feathers. Slowly, step by step, Ronda came and pressed herself close to Libby. Libby gathered her up in her arms and rocked her, still singing softly.

Mandy and James looked at each other and smiled. It was amazing to watch Ronda growing calmer and calmer.

"I think you could try now," Mr Masters said softly.

Libby didn't even turn round. She stood up carefully and carried Ronda over to the nest where she gently put her down. Ronda fluttered her wings and for an awful moment Mandy thought the hen was going to fly off. Then Ronda wriggled around and settled down. Libby backed away.

"We'll have to leave her for a while," Mr Masters said. "Just to make sure she's settled. We can't risk putting the eggs back until we're sure she's going to stay there."

"How long do we have to wait?" Libby asked.

Mr Masters ruffled her hair. "I'll try

putting them back tonight," he said. "Hens always settle better at night. We'll know in the morning if she's going to stay."

"But we won't know if the eggs are harmed?" said Mandy.

Mr Masters frowned. "We won't know for certain," he said. "Not until the weekend. The eggs should start hatching by then. Meanwhile, we'll just have to hope for the best."

"But they just *have* to be all right," Libby said desperately. "Ronda *can't* lose her chicks now – not after keeping them warm and safe for so long. And what about Nikki and Tim? I've *promised* they can adopt a chick."

Mr Masters bent down and gave her a hug. "We've done the best we can, Libby," he said. "You did a great job getting Ronda back on to the nest."

Mandy bit her lip. "And remember what you said, Libby. Ronda can have other chicks."

Libby's eyes filled with tears. "But it won't be the same," she said. "They won't be *these* chicks. They won't be her very first chicks."

9

Easter Party

Mandy and James were throwing a stick for Blackie in the back garden of Animal Ark on Saturday morning when the telephone rang.

"Mandy!" Mrs Hope called. "It's Libby for you. She sounds excited."

They looked at each other.

"It must be the chicks," James said.

Mandy nodded. "The eggs are due for hatching." She raced for the telephone.

James stood beside her as she took the call. Blackie tugged at his sleeve. The Labrador wanted to get back to their game.

"They've started to hatch!" Mandy said to James and her mum. Then she spoke into the phone. "Of course we'll come. Just as soon as we can. See you, Libby. Bye!"

"How many chicks have hatched?" James asked.

Mandy smiled. "Just one so far."

"Let's get up there fast," said James. Then he looked dismayed. "But how?"

Mrs Hope laughed. "Oh, I can think of a way!" she said. "I'll take you. And don't worry about missing anything, James. Eggs take a long time to hatch out. You'll be there all day if you wait until they're all hatched. You'd better phone your mum, and let her know where you're going."

"What about Blackie?" James said.

"We can take him, can't we, Mum?" Mandy asked.

Mrs Hope bent down and gave Blackie a pat. The Labrador looked up at her and wagged his tail.

"Just make sure he doesn't frighten Ronda," she said. "Now, are we going up to Blackheath or not?"

"You bet we are," Mandy answered, racing for the door.

But at the back of her mind there was still a worry. Were all the eggs OK? Had some of them got chilled? Would Ronda manage to hatch out all of her chicks?

"Oh, look," said Mandy softly. "Isn't it beautiful?"

The children looked in wonder at the tiny little chick as it started to emerge from the eggshell. First there was just the tiniest crack in the shell. Then the point of a beak appeared, chipping at the shell, making the hole bigger. Then a downy golden head appeared. Its bright, beady eyes blinked in the light as it looked around and its yellow coat glistened.

Ronda looked down and wriggled her body, raising her wing slightly. The chick scrabbled at the sides of its shell and, with an enormous effort, scrambled out of it altogether. For a moment it stood there uncertainly, a tiny yellow bundle. Then it scampered under Ronda's wing and the hen settled her feathers around it.

"How many does that make?" asked James.

"Three," Libby said. She peered at the nest, trying to see the chicks cuddled close under Ronda's body.

"I can hear another one tapping at the shell," James said, his ear close to the nest.

"That can go on for ages," Mandy said. "Don't you feel like giving the poor little thing a helping hand."

Libby shook her head. "Dad says the mother hen knows what to do. It's best to leave the eggs alone."

"Why don't we go and put the finishing touches to Ronda's Range?" said James.

They found Mr Masters in the back garden of the farmhouse. He was fixing the sign to the hen coop.

"Hello, there," he said. "I just thought I'd get this ready. We should be able to transfer Ronda and her chicks to it to-night. How is she getting on?"

"Three hatched out so far," Mandy

said. She looked at the coop. "That looks great, Mr Masters."

Ronda's coop looked really bright with its red paint. Mr Masters hung the notice on the post over the door. It said *Ronda's Range*.

"That's nearly as good as the Animal Ark sign," said James.

"I thought we'd set it up near the house for tonight," Mr Masters said. "We'll put it in the back garden so we can keep an eye on Ronda and her chicks."

Mandy, James and Libby helped Mr Masters to get Ronda's new home ready. Blackie was very interested in what was going on.

"Get down, Blackie," James said. "It's not for you. It's for Ronda."

They put a thick layer of paper on the floor of the coop, checked the wire netting and put the dust tray down in one corner.

"Once the coop is out in the yard they can have a proper dust-bath," Mr Masters said. "But a tray of sand and earth will do for now."

"Here's the grit box," James said.

"And don't forget the water," Mr Masters added. "We can put the food out later."

"That's perfect," said Libby as they looked at their handiwork.

Mandy frowned. "Won't the chicks be cold?" she asked. "They're so tiny."

"Don't you worry about that," Mr Masters said. "Even day-old chicks are pretty tough. And, don't forget, they've got Ronda to keep them warm. Right – time for tea!"

Mandy remembered the chicks snuggled under Ronda's warm body. It must be really cosy tucked up amongst all those feathers, she thought.

"No wonder they use feathers for quilts," she said out loud, as they went in for tea. She looked back at the coop. Soon Ronda and her little brood would be in their new home.

It was almost dark by the time all the chicks were hatched. Mandy, James and Libby waited while Mr Masters checked them. He turned to them, smiling.

"I must say you lot have done a great job here," he said. "All five of the eggs have hatched – and they're all fine healthy chicks."

"So the haybox worked," said Mandy. "They didn't get chilled."

"It's been a real success," Mr Masters said. "Now, who's going to help me move them?"

Mandy and James filled a box with fresh hay and scooped out a hollow.

"That should do," Mr Masters said. He looked at Libby. "OK," he said, "you can lift Ronda now."

Mandy reached for the Rhode Island Red and gathered her into her arms. Mandy and James stared at the chicks, fascinated. The little creatures scuttled about as the cool air struck them. Then

Mr Masters began scooping them up in his hands and transferring them to the box Mandy and James held between them.

"Now put Ronda back," he said. Libby settled the hen back on her chicks.

"Poor little things," Mandy said. "They must be wondering what's happening to them."

"They'll soon be in their nice new home," Mr Masters reassured her, as they made their way towards the farmhouse.

Mrs Masters was waiting for them. Blackie was with her.

"I've put out a good feed for Ronda," she said. "She'll need it after all her hard work."

Ronda thought so too. As soon as Mr Masters put her into the run she made for the feed dish. The chicks scampered after her, tucking themselves close around her. Blackie peered into the run, snuffling at the little yellow bodies.

"Aren't they lovely, Blackie?" James

said. "Absolutely perfect!"

The light spilled out of the back door of the farmhouse as they stood around the coop, watching Ronda and her chicks.

"Wonderful," Libby said softly. "I can't wait to tell everybody at school."

Mandy smiled. Ronda was totally caught up in her little family. She was going to be a very busy hen for a while, and wouldn't have time to mope any more.

And Libby had made friends too. She wouldn't miss Ronda while she was at school now. Her friends were just as interested in Ronda and her chicks as Libby was. It really did look as if everything had worked out perfectly.

"You know," said James. "Ronda is going to steal the show at the Easter Party."

"What?" said Libby.

James looked at her. "You haven't forgotten, have you?" he said. "I'm taking Blackie, and Laura and Jack are taking their rabbits. I thought you were taking Ronda."

"And her chicks," added Mandy.

Libby's face lit up. "I *had* forgotten," she said. She turned to her father. "Can I, Dad?" she asked. "May I take Ronda and the chicks to the Easter Party?"

Mr Masters laughed. "That's three weeks away," he said. "I reckon Ronda's chicks will be big and strong enough to stand the excitement – if you look after them."

"Oh, we will," said Libby. "Really we will!"

"Happy Easter!" Mandy called to Mrs McFarlane as they passed the post-office window on their way to the fancy dress party at school.

Mrs McFarlane waved from behind an enormous display of Easter eggs.

"Happy Easter!" Mr Hardy called back, coming out of the door of the Fox and Goose.

The whole of Welford Primary School was marching down the main street to show off their Easter costumes and masks. They were carrying baskets of Easter eggs they had collected from all the shops and houses in the village for the cottage hospital.

The school always donated Easter eggs to the hospital. Gary Roberts had been in hospital one Easter and he said it was the best Easter ever – he got so many chocolate eggs!

Mandy looked around her. Blackie was wearing a huge yellow ribbon round his neck. Laura and Jack were carrying a big wicker basket between them, and inside it their Easter bunnies were decked out in pink and blue ribbons.

Mandy moved towards Richard Tanner.

"How's Duchess?" she asked.

"She's almost back to normal now," Richard said. "I don't think you'd even notice the limp if you didn't know about it."

Mandy smiled. "And what about the kittens?" she said.

"Beautiful!" Richard said. "We've got homes for all of them. You know, if Duchess hadn't had the kittens to look after, I don't think she would have recovered so quickly."

Mandy nodded. "That's what Dad said."

"I mean, she would have been really miserable," Richard said. "But the kittens cheered her up."

Mandy looked at Libby. She, Nikki and Tim were pushing a wheelbarrow full of straw and in the middle of it were Ronda and her chicks.

"Aren't they gorgeous?" James said.

Mandy nodded. Libby looked over and waved.

"It's so wonderful," she called. "All Ronda's chicks have been adopted."

Mandy waved back. What a great Easter present, she thought. Chicks for Ronda. Chums for Libby. And chick chums for Libby's friends. Perfect! The chick challenge had had a very happy end.

LUCY DANIELS
Animal Ark Pets

0 340 67283 8	Puppy Puzzle	£2.99	❒
0 340 67284 6	Kitten Crowd	£2.99	❒
0 340 67285 4	Rabbit Race	£2.99	❒
0 340 67286 2	Hamster Hotel	£2.99	❒
0 340 68729 0	Mouse Magic	£2.99	❒
0 340 68730 4	Chick Challenge	£2.99	❒
0 340 68731 2	Pony Parade	£2.99	❒

All Hodder Children's books are available at your local bookshop or newsagent, or can be ordered direct from the publisher. Just tick the titles you want and fill in the form below. Prices and availability subject to change without notice.

Hodder Children's Books, Cash Sales Department, Bookpoint, 39 Milton Park, Abingdon, OXON, OX14 4TD, UK. If you have a credit card you may order by telephone – (01235) 831700.

Please enclose a cheque or postal order made payable to Bookpoint Ltd to the value of the cover price and allow the following for postage and packing:
UK & BFPO – £1.00 for the first book, 50p for the second book, and 30p for each additional book ordered up to a maximum charge of £3.00.
OVERSEAS & EIRE – £2.00 for the first book, £1.00 for the second book, and 50p for each additional book.

Name ....

Address ....

....

....

If you would prefer to pay by credit card, please complete:
Please debit my Visa/Access/Diner's Card/American Express (delete as applicable) card no:

Signature ....
Expiry Date ....